In the Name of Allâh, the Most Beneficent, the Most Merciful

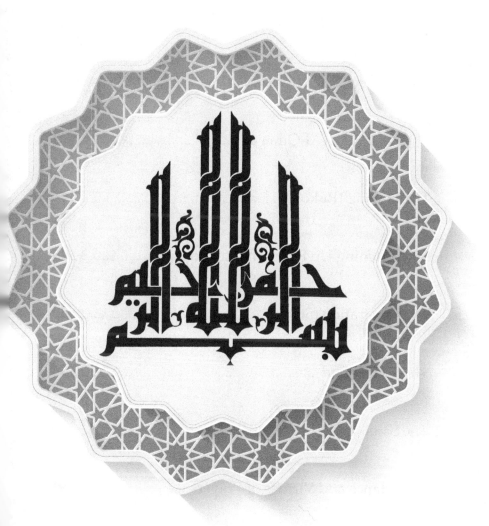

Bismi Allāhi Ar-Raĥmāni Ar-Raĥīmi

Table of Contents

Description of the Prayer

of the Prophet

THE TAKBEER
(Saying: `Allaahu Akbar')

In Arabic

اللهُ أَكْبَرُ

He begins the Prayer by saying:
Allaahu Akbar Allaah is Greater.
This is a pillar (rukn), due to his saying, "The key to the Prayer is Purification. That which makes outside actions forbidden is the takbeer, and that which causes outside actions to become permissible is the tasleem."

THE TAKBEER
(Saying: `Allaahu Akbar')

Allâhu
'Akbar

He should not raise his voice in saying the takbeer in any of the Prayers, unless he is an Imaam (leading others in prayer). It is allowed for the mu'adhdhin to repeat the takbeer of the Imaam in a louder voice in order for the people to hear it, as long as there is a need for that, such as the Imaam's being ill, having a weak voice, or there being a very large number of people praying behind him.

THE TAKBEER
(Saying: `Allaahu Akbar')

Allâh is the Most Great

The person following an Imaam in Prayer should not say the takbeer until the Imaam has finished saying it.
He should raise his hands whilst saying the takbeer or before it, or after it. All of these are established in the sunnah.

6

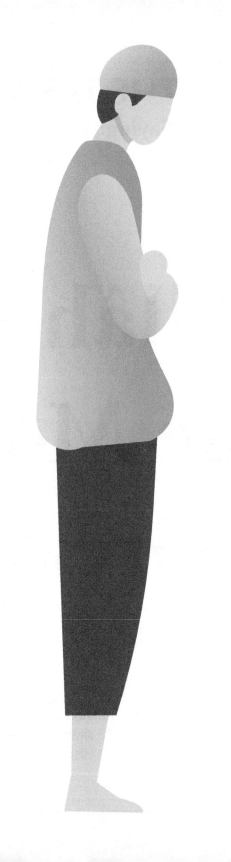

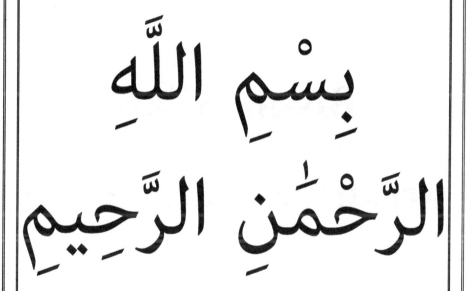

Then he recites the whole of Soorah al-Faatihah, and
(Bismillaah …) is an aayah from it. This is a pillar (rukn), and the
Prayer will not be correct without it. So it is obligatory upon even
those who do not know Arabic that they memorize it.

Bismi Allahi

arrahmani arraheem

But one who is still unable to recite it, then it is sufficient for him to say:

Subhaan-Allaah, wal-hamdulillaah, wa laa ilaaha illallaah, wallaahu Akbar, wa laa hawla wa laa quwwata illaa billaah

I declare Allaah free and far removed from all imperfections, and all praise is for Allaah, and Allaah is greater and no power except by the Will of Allah.

In the Name of Allâh,

the Most Beneficent,

the Most Merciful

It is obligatory that the one praying behind an imaam also recites it in quiet Prayers. He should also recite it in loud Prayers if he cannot hear an imaam reciting, or if it happens that the imaam remains silent after his own recitation in order to enable the follower to recite it. However, it is our view that this period of silence is not established from the Sunnah.

الْحَمْدُ لِلَّه

رَبِّ الْعَالَمِين

It is obligatory that he recites al-Faatihah in every rak'ah.
It is from the Sunnah that he sometimes recites something in
addition to it in the last two rak'ahs also.

RECITING SOORAH AL-FAATIHAH

Alhamdu lillahi

rabbi alAAalameen

All the praises and thanks be to Allâh,

the Lord of the 'Alamîn

(mankind, jinns and all that exists)

الرَّحْمٰنِ الرَّحِيمِ

Arrahmani arraheem

The Most Beneficent,

the Most Merciful

مَالِكِ

يَوْمِ الدِّينِ

RECITING SOORAH AL-FAATIHAH

Maliki yawmi addeen

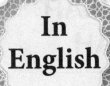

The Only Owner (and the Only Ruling Judge)

of the Day of Recompense

(i.e. the Day of Resurrection)

إِيَّاكَ نَعْبُدُ

وَإِيَّاكَ نَسْتَعِينُ

Iyyaka naAAbudu wa-iyyaka nastaAAeen

You (Alone) we worship,

and You (Alone) we ask for help

(for each and everything)

اهْدِنَا الصِّرَاطَ الْمُسْتَقِيمَ

Ihdina assirata almustaqeem

Guide us to

the Straight Way

صِرَاطَ الَّذِينَ أَنْعَمْتَ

عَلَيْهِمْ غَيْرِ الْمَغْضُوبِ

عَلَيْهِمْ وَلَا الضَّالِّينَ

Sirata allatheena anAAamta AAalayhim ghayri almaghdoobi AAalayhim wala addalleen

The Way of those on whom You have bestowed Your

Grace , not (the way) of those who earned Your Anger

(such as the Jews), nor of those who went astray

(such as the Christians)

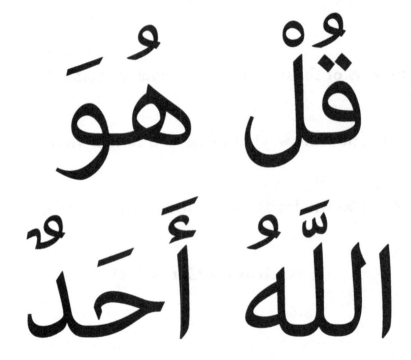

قُلْ هُوَ اللَّهُ أَحَدٌ

It is from the Sunnah that after reciting al-Faatihah, he recites another Soorah - even in the Funeral Prayer, or that he recites some aayahs, in the first two rak'ahs.

Qul huwa Allahou ahad

He may sometimes lengthen the recitation after it and shorten it at other times, due to the needs of travel, having a cough and cold, being ill or due to the crying of a child.

Say (O Muhammad

(Peace be upon him)):

"He is Allâh, (the) One.

The length of recitation will vary according to the different Prayers. So generally, the recitation in the Dawn (Fajr) Prayer is longer than the recitation in any of the other Prayers. Next comes the Zuhr, then the 'Asr and the Maghrib, then the 'Ishaa. The recitation in the (optional) Night Prayer (Salaatul-Layl) is longer than any of those.

الـلّٰـهُ

الـصَّـمَـدُ

The Sunnah is also to make the recitation in the first rak'ah longer than the recitation in the second rak'ah.
Also that he makes the recitation in the last two rak'ahs shorter than that in the first two, by about a half.

Allahou assamad

Allah is He on

Whom all depend

لَمْ يَلِدْ

وَلَمْ يُولَدْ

Lam yalid

walam youlad

He begets not,

nor is He begotten

وَلَمْ يَكُن

لَّهُ كُفُوًا أَحَدٌ

Walam yakun lahu kufuwan ahad

And there is none co-equal

or comparable unto Him

THE BOWING (RUKOO')

In Arabic

سُبْحَانَ رَبِّيَ الْعَظِيمِ

When he has finished reciting he remains silent for a moment, long enough to return his breathing to normal.

Then he raises his hands, in the manner described previously with regard to the initial takbeer.

He also says the takbeer (i.e., Allaahu Akbar), and this is obligatory.

Subhana Rabbi el-'Adim

Then he performs the rukoo' (i.e., bows) in such a manner that all his joints are settled, and each part of the body is at rest. This is a pillar (rukn).

He should place his hands firmly upon his knees. He should spread his fingers, as if he were grasping his knees. All of this is obligatory.

He should stretch out his back and make it level, such that if water were to be poured upon it, then it would settle upon it. This is an obligation.

43

THE BOWING (RUKOO')

I declare my Lord, the Supreme, free and far removed from all imperfections

He should neither cause his head to droop lower than his back, nor should he raise it above it. Rather he should make it level with his back.

He should keep his elbows (straight and) apart from his sides.

He should say in his rukoo':

Subhaana Rabbee al-'Azeem

I declare my Lord, the Supreme, free and far removed from all imperfections.

Saying it three times, or more.

44

In Arabic

سَمِعَ اللهُ

لِمَنْ حَمِدَه

Then he must raise up and straighten his back from the rukoo'.
This is a pillar.
He must say, while raising his back:
Sami' Allaahu liman hamidah
Allaah listens and responds to the one who praises Him.
This is an obligation.

46

Sami'a-Allâhu liman Hamidah

He should raise his hands when he rises up, in the manner that has preceded.

Then he should stand straight up and remain still, such that every bone returns to its place. This is a pillar.

He should say while standing:

Rabbanaa wa lakal-hamd

O our Lord! And all praise is for You.

47

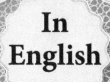
Allaah listens and responds to the one who praises Him

This is obligatory upon everyone praying, even if he is praying behind an imaam, since it is the saying prescribed for this. standing position. As for the saying, then it is the saying prescribed to be said whilst rising.

He should make this standing about as long as the rukoo' (bowing), as has preceded.

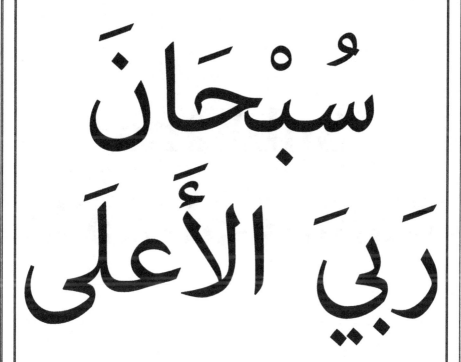

سُبْحَانَ رَبِّي الْأَعْلَى

Then he says:
Allaahu Akbar
Allaah is Greater.
and this is an obligation.
And he should raise his hands, sometimes.

Subhâna

Rabbiy-al-Aa'lâ

Then he prostrates, placing his hands upon the ground before his knees. This is what Allaah's Messenger commanded, and it is what is established from his practice. He also forbade the people from kneeling down in the manner that the camel kneels, and the camel places its knees -which are its fore-legs - first.

So when he prostrates, and it is a pillar, he should rest upon his palms, and extend together.

I declare my Lord, the Most High, free and far removed from all imperfections

He should keep his fingers them.
And point them towards the qiblah (direction of Prayer).
And he should place his palms level with his shoulders.
And sometimes he places them level with his ears.
And he must lift his elbows away from the ground. This is obligatory. He is not allowed to spread them on the ground in the manner of the dog.
He must place his nose and his forehead firmly upon the ground, this is a pillar.

In Arabic

التَّحِيَّاتُ لله

وَالصَّلَوَاتُ الطَّيَّبَاتُ

So when he finishes the second rak'ah he sits to perform the tashahhud. This is obligatory.

And he sits upon the left foot laid flat, as preceded with regard to the sitting between the two prostrations.

However it is not allowed to sit upon the two heels for this sitting.

It it is not allowed for him to sit whilst resting upon his hand, especially the left hand.

At-Tahiyyâtu Lilâhi

was-Salâwâtu

wat-Tayyibâtu

He should clench all the fingers of his right hand, placing his thumb onto his middle finger sometimes.

At other times he may make a circle with his thumb and middle finger together.

He should point his forefinger towards the qiblah (Direction of Prayer).

He should fix his gaze upon his forefinger.

And he should agitate it, making supplication with it, from the start to the end of the tashahhud.

Words of Praise and glorification

are for Allaah alone,

and Prayers and acts of worship,

and pure words and attributes

He should not point with his left forefinger.
He does all of this in every tashahhud.
The tashahhud is obligatory. If he forgets it, then he should
perform two extra prostrations for forgetfulness (Sajdatus-Sahw)
at the end of the Prayer.

السَّلامُ عَلَيْكَ أَيُّهَا النَّبِيُّ

وَرَحْمَةُ اللهِ وَبَرَكَاتُهُ

As-Salâmu ʿalayka Ayyuhan-Nabiyyu wa Rahmatu-Llâhi wa Barakâtuhu

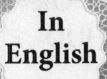
May Allaah send peace and security upon the Prophet, and may Allaah's Mercy and Blessings be upon him

السَّلامُ عَلَيْنَا وَعَلَى عِبَادِ اللهِ الصَّالِحِينَ

As-Salâmu 'Alayna

wa 'alâ-'Ibâdillâh

is-Sâlihîna

May Allaah send peace and

security upon us, and upon all

of Allaah's righteous servants

أَشْهَدُ أَنْ

لاَ إِلَهَ إِلاَّ اللهُ

Ash-hadu an lâ Ilâha Illallâhu

I bear witness that none has the right to be worshipped except Allaah

وَأَشْهَدُ أَنَّ

مُحَمَّدَاً عَبْدُهُ وَرَسُولُه

Wa ash-Hadu anna Muhammadan 'Abduhu wa Rassûluh

And I bear witness that Muhammad is His Slave and Messenger

اللَّهُمَّ صَلِّ

عَلَى مُحَمَّدٍ

وَعَلَى آلِ مُحَمَّدٍ

After this he should supplicate for blessings upon the Prophet!
saying:
Allaahumma Salli 'alaa Muhammad, wa 'alaa Aali Muhammad,
kamaa sallayta 'alaa Ibraaheem, wa 'alaa Aali Ibraaheem, innaka
Hameedun Majeed. Allaahumma baarik 'alaa Muhammad,
wa 'alaa Aali Muhammad, kamaa baarakta 'alaa Ibraaheem,
wa 'alaa Aali Ibraaheem, innaka Hameedun Majeed.

Allâhumma Salli 'ala Muhammadin wa 'ala Âli Muhammadin

O Allaah! Extol and honor Muhammad and the true followers of Muhammad, just as You extolled and honored Ibraaheem and the righteous offspring of Ibraaheem. Indeed, You are deserving of all praise, Perfect in Glory and Honor. 0 Allaah! Send continual blessings upon Muhammad and upon the true followers of Muhammad, just as You sent blessings upon Ibraaheem and upon the righteous offspring of Ibraaheem. Indeed, You are deserving of all praise, Perfect in Glory and Honor.

O Allaah! Extol and honor Muhammad and the true followers of Muhammad

In Arabic

THE WORDING FOR THE TASHAHHUD

كَمَا صَلَّيْتَ عَلَى إِبْرَاهِيمَ وَعَلَى آلِ إِبْرَاهِيمَ

Kama Sallayta 'ala Ibrâhîma wa 'ala Âli Ibrâhîma

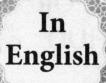
Just as You extolled and honored

Ibraaheem and the

righteous offspring of Ibraaheem

إِنَّكَ حَمِيدٌ

مَجِيدٌ

Innaka Hamîdun

Majîd

Indeed, You are deserving

of all praise, Perfect

in Glory and Honor

وَبَارِكْ عَلَى

مُحَمَّدٍ وَعَلَى

آلِ مُحَمَّدٍ

Wa Bârik 'ala Muhammadin wa 'ala Âli Muhammadin

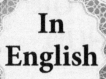
0 Allaah! Send continual blessings

upon Muhammad and upon the

true followers of Muhammad

كَمَا بَارَكْتَ عَلَى

إِبْرَاهِيمَ وَعَلَى

آلِ إِبْرَاهِيمَ

Kama Bârakta 'ala Ibrâhîma wa 'ala Âli Ibrâhîma

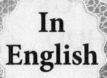

Just as You sent blessings upon

Ibraaheem and upon the righteous

offspring of Ibraaheem

إِنَّكَ حَمِيدٌ

مَجِيدٌ

Innaka Hamîdun

Majîd

Indeed, You are deserving

of all praise, Perfect

in Glory and Honor

السَّلامُ عَلَيْكُم

وَرَحمَةُ الله

Then he should give salutations to his right side, and this is a pillar, turning his face such that the whiteness of his right cheek can be seen.

He then gives salutations to his left side, turning his face such that the whiteness of his left cheek can be seen, even if it is the Funeral Prayer.

As-Salâmu 'Alaykum wa Rahmatullâh

The imaam leading others in Prayer, should raise his voice with the salutation except when performing the Funeral Prayer.

THE SALUTATION (AT-TASLEEM)

May Allaah grant you peace and security, and may His Mercy be upon you

So in conclusion I ask Allaah, the Most High, that He accepts our prayers, and the rest of our actions, and that He saves the reward of them for us on that Day when we shall meet Him.

Importance and

Virtues of Prayers

Jābir (may Allah be pleased with him) reported that the Messenger of Allah (may Allah's peace and blessings be upon him) said: "The five prayers are like a great river running by your door in which you wash five times every day."

Abu Hurayrah (may Allah be pleased with him) reported: I heard the Messenger of Allah (may Allah's peace and blessings be upon him) say: "What if there was a river at the door of anyone of you wherein he takes a bath five times daily, would there remain any of his filth?" They said: "Nothing of his filth would remain." He said: "This is similar to the five prayers by means of which Allah erases sins."

Explanation

The Prophet (may Allah's peace and blessings be upon him) likened abstract filth to physical filth. Just as bathing five times a day removes filth, praying five times a day eliminates sins.

Abu Hurayrah (may Allah be pleased with him) reported that the Prophet (may Allah's peace and blessings be upon him) said: "The five (daily) prayers, and Friday prayer to the next Friday prayer, and Ramadan to the next Ramadan, are expiation of the sins committed in between them, so long as major sins are avoided."

Explanation

The five daily prayers expiate the sins committed between them except the major sins. Similarly, the sins committed between Friday prayer and the next Friday prayer are expiated apart from major sins, and the same applies to fasting in Ramadan and fasting in the next Ramadan.

Jundub ibn 'Abdullāh (may Allah be pleased with him) reported: The Messenger of Allah (may Allah's peace and blessings be upon him) said: "Whoever performs the Fajr prayer is under the protection of Allah, so none of you should harm the one under the protection of Allah in any way, for whoever does that will be definitely overtaken by the wrath of Allah and will then be thrown on his face in Hellfire."

Whoever performs the Fajr prayer enters under the protection of Allah, as if he has entered into a covenant with Allah that no one will harm him. It is unlawful then to harm such a person, because harming him will be considered transgression against Allah, and a violation of the protection that Allah has granted this person. Whoever breaks the covenant of Allah and transgresses against Him exposes himself to His wrath, and Allah will retaliate against him for harming someone who is under His protection.

Abu ʿAbdullah Jābir ibn ʿAbdullah al-Ansāri (may Allah be pleased with him and his father) reported that a man asked the Messenger of Allah (may Allah's peace and blessings be upon him): "Tell me, if I were to pray the obligatory prayers, fast Ramadan, deem lawful all that has been made lawful, and deem unlawful all that has been made unlawful, without increasing anything on that, would I enter Paradise?" The Prophet (may Allah's peace and blessings be upon him) said: "Yes."

Explanation

Abu 'Abdullah Jābir ibn 'Abdullah al-Ansāri (may Allah be pleased with him and his father) reported that a man asked the Messenger of Allah (may Allah's peace and blessings be upon him): "Tell me, if I were to pray the obligatory prayer (i.e. the five obligatory prayers, and would not perform any extra voluntary prayers), fast Ramadan (only without any voluntary fasts), deem lawful all that has been made lawful (and do only what is permissible), and deem unlawful all that has been made unlawful (and avoid all that, believing in its prohibition and finding sufficiency in what is lawful), without increasing anything on that, would I enter Paradise (is this adequate for entering Paradise?)" The Prophet (may Allah's peace and blessings be upon him) answered in the affirmative because piety entails doing the obligations and avoiding the prohibitions. This is what textual proofs define as 'Moqtasid' or moderate, which refers to the one who performs only what Allah has made obligatory for him and avoid only what He has prohibited.

Abu Hurayrah (may Allah be pleased with him) reported that the Messenger of Allah (may Allah's peace and blessings be upon him) said: "The most burdensome prayers for the hypocrites are the 'Ishā and Fajr prayers. If they were to know the virtue of them, they would come to them even if they had to crawl. I sometimes thought of ordering for the prayer to be commenced, and I would appoint a man to lead the people in prayer, and then I would go, along with some men having bundles of firewood, to the people who are not attending the prayer and burn their houses with fire upon them."

Explanation

The hypocrites used to show off and rarely remember Allah, the Almighty, as revealed in the Qur'an. Their laziness appears most significantly in the 'Ishā' and Fajr prayers because they are offered under the cover of darkness, when people will not see them. Most hypocrites neglect to offer these two prayers, which are performed during the times of rest and sleep. Only those driven by faith and the pursuit of reward in the Hereafter are keen on observing them. Hence, the Fajr and 'Ishā' prayers are the most difficult for the hypocrites.

If they knew the great reward of offering these two prayers along with the Muslim congregation in the mosque, they would come to them, even if they had to crawl upon their hands and knees, just like babies. The Prophet (may Allah's peace and blessings be upon him) swore that he had actually thought of punishing those who lazily fail to attend these two prayers in congregation. He determined to order the prayer be commenced and let someone else lead it and then go, along with a group of men carrying bundles of firewood, and set fire to the houses of those who did not attend the congregational prayer, due to the gravity of their action. Yet, he subsequently decided against it, since those houses lodged innocent women and children who had done no wrong, as mentioned in some versions of the Hadīth.

Abu Mālik Al-Hārith ibn al-Ash'ari (may Allah be pleased with him) reported: "The Messenger of Allah (may Allah's peace and blessings be upon him) said: 'Purity is half of the Imān, Al-Hamdu Lillāh [All praise be to Allah] fills the Scale, and Subhān Allah wal-Hamdu Lillāh [Exalted is Allah and all praise be to Allah] fills what is between the heavens and the earth. Prayer is light, charity is proof, patience is radiance, and the Qur'an is proof either for you or against you. Every person goes out in the morning and sells his soul; he either saves it from doom or throws it into destruction.'"

The Messenger of Allah (may Allah's peace and blessings be upon him) said that purity is half of Imān. It refers to the inward and outward purity. The purity of the body is achieved by keeping away from filth and removing Hadath (state of ritual impurity). The purity of the heart is to be free from polytheism and diseases of the heart. Half of the Imān: means half of the prayer, since prayer is not accepted without purity. He also said that Al-hamdu Lillāh (All praise be to Allah) fills the Scale, as it involves describing

Allah Almighty by all of His perfect and glorious attributes along with loving and extolling Him. This statement fills the Scale by which the deeds are weighed. Subhān Allah (Exalted is Allah) is meant for exalting Allah above all that does not befit Him from defects and resemblance to His creation. Subhān Allah and/or (this uncertainty is by the narrator) Al-hamdu Lillāh fills what is between heaven and earth for a distance covered in five hundred years. This is out of the limitless favor of Allah. Prayer is light: light in the worldly life and light for the servant on the Day of Judgment. Charity is proof as it decisively proves the truthfulness of the servant's faith, given the fact that one is naturally born with loving wealth. So, giving out such wealth willingly is undoubtedly a decisive proof of the truthfulness of one's Imān. Patience, in its three forms, is radiance: patience for performing acts of obedience, patience for shunning disobedience, and patience for the painful predestination. It illuminates the way before the servant. The Qur'an is proof either for or against you. The Qur'an is the word of Allah that He sent down upon His Prophet (may Allah's peace and blessings be upon him) through Jibrīl, kept between the two sides of the Mus-haf's cover. When one recites it, it is as if he is speaking to the Most Merciful. It can be proof for you when you have faith in it, believe in all that is stated in it, comply with its commands, and avoid its prohibition. But, if you learn and memorize it, then you, indulging in rest and sleep, abandon it, leave prayer, and act contrary to its commands and prohibitions, it becomes proof against you. "Every person goes out in the morning": When it is morning, all people go about in the land in pursuit of provision. However, some do this for the good of themselves while others for their destruction. They sell themselves in the sense that they get their selves engaged in actions. So, you would either sell yourself to Allah Almighty and save it from His Fire or sell it to the devil by committing sins, crimes, and evildoing, whereby you lead it to its destruction in Hellfire.

'Abdullāh ibn Mas'ūd (may Allah be pleased with him) reported: I asked the Prophet (may Allah's peace and blessings be upon him): "Which deed is dearest to Allah?" He said: "Offering prayer at the appointed time." I said: "Then, what comes next?" He said: "Dutifulness to one's parents." I said: "Then, what comes next?" He said: "Jihad in the way of Allah." These were the things the Messenger of Allah (may Allah's peace and blessings be upon him) said to me, and if I had asked him for more, he would have given me more.

Ibn Mas'ūd (may Allah be pleased with him) asked the Prophet (may Allah's peace and blessings be upon him) about the acts of worship, as to which of them is dearest to Allah, the Almighty. The dearest an act to Allah, the greatest its reward will be.

The Prophet (may Allah's peace and blessings be upon him) clarified that the dearest act to Allah is offering the obligatory prayer at the appointed time which was prescribed by the Almighty Legislator. This is because in doing so a slave actually hastens to answer the call of his Lord, obey His command, and observes this important obligation.

Out of his desire to attain goodness, Ibn Mas'ūd (may Allah be pleased with him) did not stop at that point; rather, he asked him about the deed that falls in the next degree, and the Prophet (may Allah's peace and blessings be upon him) replied that being dutiful to one's parents comes next.

So, the first deed is an exclusive right of Allah, and the next one is an exclusive right of parents, and it directly follows the right of Allah. Moreover, attaching great importance to this right, Allah, the Almighty, associates the duty to show kindness and obedience to one's parents along with His Oneness in numerous places in the noble Qur'an. Indeed, a person's parents deserve this right in return for being the means of his existence and for bringing him up, feeding him, and showing him love and affection.

Then, Ibn Mas'ūd (may Allah be pleased with him) asked the Prophet (may Allah's peace and blessings be upon him) about the act falling in the next degree within this series of virtuous deeds. The Prophet replied: "Jihad in the way of Allah." In fact, Jihad is the highest peak in Islam and its pillar without which it would not stand, and through it the word of Allah rises and His religion spreads.

If Jihad were to be abandoned – Allah forbid – Islam would be destroyed and Muslims would decline and their glory, sovereignty, power, and sovereignty would go away and vanish.

Jihad is a confirmed obligation on every Muslim. If a Muslim does not participate in Jihad or did not have a thought of going for it, he will die while being guilty of some kind of hypocrisy.

Jarīr ibn Abdullāh (may Allah be pleased with him) reported: I gave the Messenger of Allah (may Allah's peace and blessings be upon him) pledge to establish the prayer, pay Zakah, and advise every Muslim.

Explanation

Jarīr (may Allah be pleased with him) said: "I gave the Prophet (may Allah's peace and blessings be upon him) pledge to perform prayer, pay Zakah, and give good advice to every Muslim." The pledge given here means a covenant. It was called a pledge because both parties extend their hands and hold them together as they do in pledges. These three things represent: 1. An absolute right of Allah. 2. An absolute right of the human being. 3. A common right. The absolute right of Allah is "to establish prayer", which means performing the prayer in the manner required by offering it in its due time, fulfilling all of its pillars, obligations, and conditions, and perfecting it with its recommended acts. Establishment of prayer for men requires performing it in the mosque with the congregation. It is also required that prayer is offered with an attentive heart and heedful mind that understands what is being said and done. This is, in fact, very important because it is the locus and soul of the prayer. The absolute right of humans is to "pay Zakah", which means giving Zakah to its proper recipients who deserve it. The common right is to "advise every Muslim". This includes the Muslim who is relative or non-relative, old or young, and male or female. The way in which a person should give advice to every Muslim is demonstrated in the Hadīth reported by Anas (may Allah be pleased with him) which reads: "None of you becomes a true believer until he loves for his brother what he loves for himself." This is the essence of advice. In other words, a Muslim should love for his brothers what he loves for himself to the extent that what pleases them makes him pleased and what saddens them makes him sad. One should also treat others in the way he wishes to be treated. Indeed, there are many examples falls under this category.

Thawbān (may Allah be pleased with him) reported that the Prophet (may Allah's peace and blessings be upon him) said: "Make frequent prostration to Allah, for every prostration that you make for Allah, He will raise your position a degree and will remit one of your sins."

The context of this Hadīth: Ma'dān ibn Talhah (may Allah have mercy upon him) said: "I went to Thawbān and said: Tell me of an action which if I perform it, Allah will admit me into Paradise" or he said: "Tell me what the most beloved deeds to Allah are." Thawbān was silent, so he asked him again. Thawbān remained silent, so he asked him for the third time and he answered: "I asked the Messenger of Allah (may Allah's peace and blessings be upon him) about this and he said: 'Make frequent prostration...'" (the

Hadīth ends with: ' Ma'dān said: "I later met Abu Ad-Dardā' and asked him the same question, and he gave me the same answer as Thawbān." "Make frequent prostration" means be keen on frequent prostration. This is similar to the Hadīth reported by Rabī'ah ibn Ka'b al-Aslami (may Allah be pleased with him) who said to the Prophet (may Allah's peace and blessings be upon him): "I ask seek your companionship in Paradise." So the Prophet responded saying: "Then help me achieve this by making frequent prostration (to Allah)." Also, 'Ubādah ibn As-Sāmit (may Allah be pleased with him) said that he heard the

Messenger of Allah (may Allah's peace and blessings be upon him) saying: "No one prostrates to Allah but Allah will record one good reward for him, and will erase thereby one bad deed, and raise him in status one degree, so make frequent prostration." Prostration to Allah is one of the best acts of obedience, and one of the most sublime ways to get closer to Allah because of the ultimate humility and servitude to Allah that it represents. Prostration involves placing the highest and noblest part of one's body, which is his face, on the dusty ground which people tread on and treat with disrespect. It is noteworthy to mention that prostration here means: prostration within the prayer, not prostration per se. Prostration alone is not permissible because it was not legislated in the Qur'an or Sunnah. The fundamental principle regarding acts of worship is that they are impermissible to perform except if there is proof (from the Qur'an or Sunnah) that they are legislated. Hence, prostration outside prayer is impermissible except for a legislated reason such as the prostration of recitation required when reading certain verses in the Qur'an or the prostration of thankfulness to Allah. These two types of prostration have evidence in Islamic Shariah. Then the Prophet (may Allah's peace and blessings be upon him) clarified the extent of reward that the person receives when he prostrates. He attains two great rewards: 1. Allah raises his status one rank, meaning that he will be raised in the sight of Allah, as well as in the hearts of people and in his record of good deeds. 2. Allah erases one sin from his record of bad deeds. A person reaches perfection by removing what he dislikes and achieving what he likes. The raising of one's status is what man likes, and sins are among what he dislikes. If his status is raised by one rank and one sin is erased from his record, then he, indeed, has received what he loves and was saved from what he fears.

Abu Mūsa al-Ash‘ari (may Allah be pleased with him) reported that the Messenger of Allah (may Allah's peace and blessings be upon him) said: "Whoever prays the Bardayn will enter Paradise."

Meaning of this Hadīth: Regular performance of these two prayers is a means of entering Paradise. The term 'Bardayn' refers to the Fajr and 'Asr prayers. Proof of that is the statement of the Prophet (may Allah's peace and blessings be upon him) in the Hadīth reported by Jarīr: "Prayer before the sun rises and before it sets." In a narration by Muslim, he added: "The 'Asr and Fajr prayers." Then Jarīr recited the verse: {and glorify the praises of your Lord before the rising of the sun, and before its setting}. They were called 'Bardayn' (the two cool ones) because they are performed at the cool times of the day, which are its two ends when the air is pleasant and the intensity of the heat is gone. Many Hadīths indicated the virtue of these two prayers, including what was reported by 'Umārah ibn Ru'aybah from his father that the Prophet (may Allah's peace and blessings be upon him) said: "Whoever prays before sunrise and before it sets, does not enter Hellfire." These two prayers were specifically mentioned because the time of the Fajr prayer is when one enjoys the sweetness of sleep; and the time of the 'Asr prayer is when one is preoccupied with finishing off his daytime chores and his trade. Performing these two prayers despite that is a proof of one's freedom of laziness and his love of worship. This entails performing all the other prayers. If one observes these two prayers regularly, then he will be more observant of the other prayers. Specifying these two prayers does not mean that whoever prays them apart from the rest of the five obligatory prayers enters Paradise, as this is contrary to the textual evidence. The statement of the Prophet (may Allah's peace and blessings be upon him): "Whoever prays the Bardayn…" means praying them in the enjoined manner, i.e. praying them on time, and if he is a man then he should pray them in congregation since congregational prayer is obligatory, and it is impermissible for a man to abandon congregational prayer in the mosque while he is capable of it.

Supplications

After Obligatory Prayers

Repeat 3 times:

أَسْتَغْفِرُ اللهُ

Astaghfirullah

(I ask Allah for forgiveness.)

اللَّهُمَّ أَنْتَ السَّلَامُ، وَمِنْكَ السَّلَامُ، تَبَارَكْتَ يَا ذَا الجَلَالِ وَالإِكْرَامِ.

Allahumma AntasSalam, Wa MinkasSalam, Tabarakta Yaa Dhal Jalali Wal ikraam.

O Allah! You are Peace, and peace comes from You. Blessed You are, O possessor of Glory and Honor.

لَا إِلهَ إِلَّا اللهُ وَحْدَهُ لَا شَرِيكَ لَهُ، لَهُ الْمُلْكُ وَلَهُ الْحَمْدُ وَهُوَ عَلَى كُلِّ شَيْءٍ قَدِيرٌ.

La ilaha ilalah Wahdahu La Sherika Lah, Lahul Mulku, Wa Lahul Hamd, Wa Huwa 'Ala Kulli Shay'in Qadir.

None has the right to be worshiped except Allah, alone, without any partner, to Him belongs all sovereignty and praise and He is over all things omnipotent.

اللهم اعني على ذكرك وشكرك وحسن
عبادتك.

*Alahumma a'innee ala dhikrika
wa shukrika wa husni E'baadatik.*

O Allah, help me in remembering
You, and in being grateful to You, and
in worshiping You properly.

Repeat Each 33 Times:

سُبْحَانَ اللَّه

Subhaanal-Laah

(Glory be to Allah.)

الحَمْدُ لله

Alhamdu lil-laah

(Praise is to Allah.)

اللَّه أَكْبَرُ

Allahu Akbar

(Allah is the Greatest.)

And Then Say Once:

لَا إِلٰهَ إِلَّا اللهُ وَحْدَهُ لَا شَرِيكَ لَهُ، لَهُ الْمُلْكُ وَلَهُ الْحَمْدُ وَهُوَ عَلَى كُلِّ شَيْءٍ قَدِيرٌ.

La ilaha ilalah Wahdahu La Sherika Lah, Lahul Mulku, Wa Lahul Hamd, Wa Huwa 'Ala Kulli Shay'in Qadir.

None has the right to be worshiped except Allah, alone, without any partner, to Him belongs all sovereignty and praise and He is over all things omnipotent.

Recite Ayatul Kursy (Surah Al Baqara 2:255)

اللَّهُ لاَ إِلَهَ إِلاَّ هُوَ الْحَيُّ الْقَيُّومُ لاَ تَأْخُذُهُ سِنَةٌ وَلاَ نَوْمٌ لَهُ مَا فِي السَّمَاوَاتِ وَمَا فِي الأَرْضِ مَنْ ذَا الَّذِي يَشْفَعُ عِنْدَهُ إِلاَّ بِإِذْنِهِ يَعْلَمُ مَا بَيْنَ أَيْدِيهِمْ وَمَا خَلْفَهُمْ وَلاَ يُحِيطُونَ بِشَيْءٍ مِنْ عِلْمِهِ إِلاَّ بِمَا شَاءَ وَسِعَ كُرْسِيُّهُ السَّمَاوَاتِ وَالأَرْضَ وَلاَ يَئُودُهُ حِفْظُهُمَا وَهُوَ الْعَلِيُّ الْعَظِيمُ.

Allahu laaa ilaaha illaa huwal haiyul qai-yoom; laa taakhuduhoo sinatunw wa laa nawm; lahoo maa fissamaawaati wa maa fil ard; man dalladee yashfa'u indahooo illaa be idhnih; ya'lamu maa baina aideehim wa maa khalfahum; wa laa yuheetoona beshai 'immin 'ilmihee illa be maa

141

shaaaa; wasi'a kursiyyuhus samaa

waati wal arda wa la ya'ooduho

hifduhumaa; wa huwal aliyyul

'adheem.

(Allah — there is no God but He, the Living, the Self-Subsisting and All-Sustaining. Slumber seizes Him not, nor sleep. To Him belongs whatsoever is in the heavens and whatsoever is in the earth. Who is he that will intercede with Him except by His permission? He knows what is before them and what is behind them; and they encompass nothing of His knowledge except what He pleases. His knowledge extends over the heavens and the earth; and the care of them burdens Him not; and He

is the High, the Great.)

Recite Surah al-Ikhlas (once)

بسم الله الرحمن الرحيم

قُلْ هُوَ اللَّهُ أَحَدٌ ﴿١﴾ اللَّهُ الصَّمَدُ ﴿٢﴾ لَمْ يَلِدْ وَلَمْ يُولَدْ ﴿٣﴾ وَلَمْ يَكُن لَّهُ كُفُوًا أَحَدٌ ﴿٤﴾

Bismillaahir Rahmaanir Raheem
(1) Qul huwal laahu ahad; (2) Allah
hus-samad; (3) Lam yalid wa lam
yoolad; (4) Wa lam yakul-lahu kufuwan
ahad.

In the name of God, Most
Gracious, Most Merciful
(1) Say: He is Allah, the One and Only;
(2) Allah, the Eternal, Absolute; (3) He
begetteth not, nor is He begotten; (4)
And there is none like unto Him.

Recite Surah al-Falaq (once)

بِسْمِ اللهِ الرَّحْمَنِ الرَّحِيْمِ

قُلْ أَعُوذُ بِرَبِّ الْفَلَقِ ﴿١﴾ مِن شَرِّ مَا خَلَقَ ﴿٢﴾ وَمِن شَرِّ غَاسِقٍ إِذَا وَقَبَ ﴿٣﴾ وَمِن شَرِّ النَّفَّاثَاتِ فِي الْعُقَدِ ﴿٤﴾ وَمِن شَرِّ حَاسِدٍ إِذَا حَسَدَ ﴿٥﴾

Bismillaahir Rahmaanir Raheem
(1) Qul a'uzoo bi rabbil-falaq; (2) Min sharri ma khalaq; (3) Wa min sharri ghasiqin iza waqab; (4) Wa min sharrin-naffaa-saati fil 'uqad; (5) Wa min shar ri haasidin iza hasad.

In the name of God, Most Gracious, Most Merciful
(1) Say: I seek refuge with the Lord of the Dawn; (2) From the mischief of created things; (3) From the mischief of

145

Darkness as it overspreads; (4) From the mischief of those who practice secret arts; (5) And from the mischief of the envious one as he practices envy.

Recite Surah An-Nas (once)

بِسْمِ اللهِ الرَّحْمنِ الرَّحِيمِ

قُلْ أَعُوذُ بِرَبِّ النَّاسِ ﴿١﴾ مَلِكِ النَّاسِ ﴿٢﴾ إِلَهِ النَّاسِ ﴿٣﴾ مِن شَرِّ الْوَسْوَاسِ الْخَنَّاسِ ﴿٤﴾ الَّذِي يُوَسْوِسُ فِي صُدُورِ النَّاسِ ﴿٥﴾ مِنَ الْجِنَّةِ وَ النَّاسِ ﴿٦﴾

Bismillaahir Rahmaanir Raheem
(1) Qul a'uzu birabbin naas; (2)
Malikin naas; (3) Ilaahin naas; (4) Min
sharril was waasil khannaas; (5) Al
lazee yuwas wisu fee sudoorin naas; (6)
Minal jinnati wan naa.

In the name of God, Most
Gracious, Most Merciful
(1) Say: I seek refuge with the Lord and
Cherisher of Mankind, (2) The King (or
Ruler) of Mankind, (3) The Allah (for

judge) of Mankind,- (4) From the mischief of the Whisperer (of Evil), who withdraws (after his whisper),- (5) (The same) who whispers into the hearts of Mankind,- (6) Among Jinns and among men.

Recite the above three Suras 3 times after Fajr & Maghrib..

لَا إِلٰهَ إِلَّا اللّٰهُ وَحْدَهُ لَا شَرِيكَ لَهُ، لَهُ الْمُلْكُ وَلَهُ الْحَمْدُ وَهُوَ عَلَى كُلِّ شَيْءٍ قَدِيرٌ.

La ilaha ilalah Wahdahu La Sherika Lah, Lahul Mulku, Wa Lahul Hamd, Wa Huwa 'Ala Kulli Shay'in Qadir.

None has the right to be worshiped except Allah, alone, without any partner, to Him belongs all sovereignty and praise and He is over all things omnipotent.

Repeat 10 times after Fajr & Maghrib.

Made in the USA
Las Vegas, NV
20 November 2023

81204082R00085